# Monday Motivations

*52 weeks to a more purposful you.*

# Monday Motivations

## 52 weeks to a more purposeful you.

by

### Corry Ann March

Inspired

A DIVISION OF CIVITAS PRESS

# Contents

## Dedication

Dedicated to my brothers, Joshua & Kaleb. You have both influenced and inspired me more than you know. Thank you for loving me and supporting me.

## Acknowledgements

*"Each person represents a world in us, a world possibly not born until they arrive, and it is only by this meeting that a new world is born." ~ Anaïs Nin*

A heartfelt appreciation to:

My husband, Stephen March, you have showed me more loving, kindness than I knew possible. You cease to amaze and inspire me. Your love, support, and strength have contributed tremendously to me, the children and in creating the life of our dreams. You are my favorite person!

My children, Skylar and Jayden. There are no words great enough to express my love and appreciation to you. Thank you for giving me writing time and purpose. You are proof of God's divine love, creativity, and energy.

My parents. You have given me every thing needed to create a beautiful and fulfilling life- unconditional love and faith in God. You have demonstrated and inspired me to build a life of freedom, authenticity and creativity. I love you so much!

Traci Bachetti, since the day we met you have been contributing to my life in so many ways. Thank you for being so generous to me with your time, support, encouragement, ideas, resources and more. You are a cherished friend.

David Ramos, you have given me so much. I appreciate you for all the learning and character building you have given me, and most valuably, our children. I am forever grateful to have you in my life.

All those who have participated to putting this book together- Brittany Gregory, thank you for all the editing and for your faith in me. Diane March, thanks for your continued praise and support and for the time you spent editing. Jonathan Brink, thank you for taking in the vision for this project and for all the mentoring you have freely shared in the process.

To all those not individually mentioned, my friends, family, clients coaches, teachers, mentors and colleagues- the quote from Anaïs Nin says it perfectly. I am able to love my life and give back to others because of you. Every conversation and every experience I have shared with you has shaped my perspectives, my growth, and my abilities. Thank you for your unique imprint on this earth and for your inspiration in my life!

# Introduction

Life isn't perfect, nor is it easy, but it can be enjoyable, fulfilling and purposeful if we choose to create it to be so. *Monday Motivations* is a quick and easy way to help you create the rich and fulfilling life you desire. All of our lives are busy and squeezing in another 250-page book isn't feasible for every one. I myself am a very slow reader, so I wanted to give others an obtainable read that would be effective and progressive in helping them create a positive outlook and a possibility mindset. *Monday Motivations* is purposefully designed to take no more than 15 minutes a week.

There are 52 reads, one for each week of the year. You can choose to either start with Week 1 or start with whatever week of the year it is. Each and every week, read just one section. I've also provide a short journaling section for each read to give you the space to put down your thoughts. Many of the weeks have exercises or assignments in there, to deepen your learning and broaden your perspective. Journaling these exercises, along with the aha's that come up during your week, will increase the impact this weekly devotional has on your mindset and outlook.

What you can expect from reading *Monday Motivations* is increased awareness of what YOU CAN DO with your current situation. Your sense of empowerment will expand. Fears, doubts and worries will vaporize, and you will see more possibilities every day. You can look forward to the rewards that come with taking action on your hopes and dreams.

My desire for you is that at the end of a year, 52 weeks, you will have gained more ground in unleashing your vision and reaching your full potential and you will inspire others around you to do the same.

Sending love and appreciation to you for your unique, one of a kind purpose, on this earth.

Corry Ann March

Allow a possibility mindset to
carve out a new path for your life.

# 1. POSSIBILITY

*"Stop thinking in terms of limitations and start thinking in terms of possibilities."* ~Terry Josephson

When an obstacle shows up in your life, the way you look at it will determine what you get from it. Whatever you believe will be your truth. If you believe something is impossible that will be the truth. It will be impossible. Your mind will hold your belief as factual and will create blinders, limiting you from seeing anything contrary. However, if you believe something is possible your mind will be open and able to see possibilities. You will be able to see opportunity and solutions will show up. Possibility will be your truth.

Most people determine whether or not something is possible by their ability to see "how" it is going to happen. If they can see the "how," they think it is possible. If they don't see the "how," they believe it's impossible. The need to know how creates a far too narrow path for possibilities and solutions. It is simply limiting and it cultivates mediocrity and stagnancy.

So, where are you at today? What obstacle, are you faced with and how do you see that challenge? What do you believe about your difficult situation? Recognize that you do not need to know "how" it is going to work out. However, you do need to believe that it is possible.

Test it out. Take notice when you believe something is impossible. Recognize when your mind shuts down possibility. Then ask yourself, "What if it was possible?" Ponder on that question for a while. Allow the possibility thinking to do its work and watch how creativity, opportunity, and expectancy show up. Possibility thinking will carve out a new path that you had not seen before.

CHOOSE TODAY to believe that ANYTHING IS POSSIBLE.

# My Journal

*Try out alternative perspectives and
watch the possibilities unfold.*

# 2. PERSPECTIVE

*"Few people have the imagination for reality." ~ Goethe*

For most of us, we would prefer to be in a place of certainty. We would like to see where we are going and have surety that we are going to get there. We want to know who is going with us. Not knowing and not seeing can be a very vulnerable place.

Try this quick exercise. Close your eyes and walk around your house for a few minutes and do a routine task. When you do this, you may experience emotions of perplexity and frustration, even though you are in a place of familiarity. Do this same exercise in a place you are not familiar with and the emotions may increase to stress, fear, and anxiety.

That's what it's like in our lives when we lack vision. Vision can be blurred or lost due to a change that we have initiated or that has been thrown our way. It can feel scary in these places of uncertainty, when our sight is compromised. The normal response to loss of vision is fear and panic, a frantic scurry to get sight back and re-create familiarity. When sight is lost and fear strikes we often make decisions coming from a fight and flight energy and do things contrary to what our heart is telling us.

So, what can we do in these times of uncertainty, when our vision is blurred and our sight is compromised? How can we best respond when we are feeling frustration, fear, and stress? STOP-pause. Take a moment to access visibility by getting to a higher vantage point where you can see various perspectives. To do this, recognize where you are. Turn your attention inside. What are the thoughts you are having from this current perspective, in the land of the unknown? Physically get up and move to a different place and pretend you are looking at the situation from another point of view, maybe from the point of view of another person, not affected by the situation. What are the thoughts from that perspective? Now try a future perspective, after this time has past. What would those thoughts be? Do this with as many different perspectives as you can think of, from a child's perspective, from your best friend's perspective. By identifying some other points of view, you will experience release and the situation won't seem so tight because you will begin to see other options and other possibilities. The key is to STOP and identify some other perspectives and the realities that are in those different perspectives.

No matter what situation you are in today, wherever your vision may have blurred or have been blinded, you can find a place of improved perspective, if you are willing to step out of your current viewpoint and into alternative viewpoints. Your options and possibilities are limitless, if you will open up to seeing them. I encourage you today to get up and move. Pick 5 or more different perspectives and write about what your situation looks like from those perspectives. In finding other viewpoints, possibilities will unfold.

# My Journal

_____

_____

_____

_____

_____

_____

_____

_____

_____

_____

_____

_____

_____

_____

_____

_____

_____

_____

*Keep your thoughts in check.*

# 3. THOUGHT-LIFE

*"We are not our feelings. We are not our moods. We are not even our thoughts."* ~ *Stephen R. Covey*

We are not our thoughts. Thoughts come to us, but they're not always from us. Though we cannot control thoughts coming to us, we can decide what we do with them. It starts by being aware of them.

I'll share with you a personal experience that conveys just how irrational our thoughts can be, if left unchecked. It's actually quite embarrassing, but since I am not my thoughts, I'll go ahead and share.

I received an e-mail promoting an event and the photo of the keynote speaker captured my attention. Though the speaker was well dressed and had a great smile, it wasn't her beauty that caught my eye. What intrigued me most was the fact that she had no arms. As I read her bio, I learned she was a pilot, has a black belt in Taekwondo, recently learned how to surf, and is an exceptionally inspiring speaker.

I initially felt motivated by her story, but that inspiration quickly disappeared. In a split second I felt discouraged and when I questioned that discouragement, I realized a fleeting thought had created the change in emotion. The thought was so quick and quiet and it said, "I could never be that inspirational because I have arms." Now that is just outright ridiculous. When I realized what the thought was, I literally laughed out loud.

It was an irrational thought, but no more irrational than any other limiting belief that stops us from taking action on a dream. We have all experienced thoughts that come to us, telling us why we can't be, do or have what we want. "I don't have an education, I'm too old, I'm too young, I don't have enough money, I have too much money, I don't have enough experience, my upbringing was too sheltered, my upbringing was too dysfunctional"…and the list goes on.

Whatever thoughts you have heard as to why you can't be, do, or have what you want, just know, they are just thoughts. They are not you. You get to decide what you do with those thoughts. Keep your thought life in check and choose what thoughts you will believe.

# My Journal

_____

_____

_____

_____

_____

_____

_____

_____

_____

_____

_____

_____

_____

_____

_____

_____

_____

_____

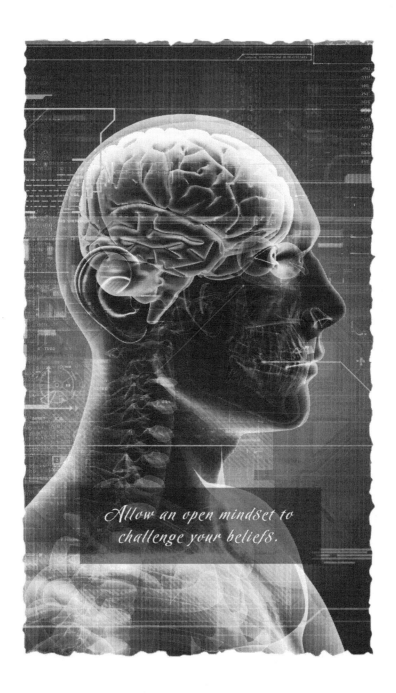

*Allow an open mindset to challenge your beliefs.*

# 4. BELIEFS

*"This is how humans are: we question all our beliefs, except for the ones we really believe, and those we never think to question."* ~ *Orson Scott Card*

A belief is any story we hold as true, whether we are aware of it or not.

Sometimes our beliefs are accurate and sometimes they are inaccurate. Regardless of their accuracy, we hold them as factual. Our beliefs create our emotions. Our emotions develop into moods and attitudes. And our moods and attitudes influence our decisions and our actions. Ultimately, beliefs create our reality.

Where do our beliefs come from? Though others can influence us, outside influences do not create our beliefs. We create our beliefs. We create our beliefs by the thoughts we have about an experience. This is why beliefs can vary greatly from person to person. There could be a dozen people in the same location, at the same time, involved with the same occurrence and you will hear 12 different stories, 12 different experiences. Whose story is accurate? Each person holds his or her own story as true, so it is subjective.

So, what do we do with our beliefs to ensure they are true and that they are working for us? We question them. We challenge them. Recognize a belief you are holding now right now about your current situation. Write it down and then ask yourself, "Is that belief true? Is it a fact or what else could possibly be true?" By simply questioning our beliefs, we open up our ability to entertain other possible truths. This willingness creates an open mindset, which is needed for growth.

Choose today to create an open mindset, necessary for growth by questioning your beliefs. When you do this possibilities are created and growth is certain. Don't get stuck in your current belief system, grow out of it and into beliefs that support your goals and dreams.

# My Journal

_____

_____

_____

_____

_____

_____

_____

_____

_____

_____

_____

_____

_____

_____

_____

_____

_____

Pay attention to what you
give your attention to.

# 5. ATTENTION

*"Choice of attention - to pay attention to this and ignore that - is to the inner life what choice of action is to the outer. In both cases, a man is responsible for his choice and must accept the consequences, whatever they may be."* ~ W. H. Auden

Attention is like a magnet. It will draw in whatever you give your attention to. Therefore, pay attention to what you pay attention to. Your attention is going to be on something, whether you are purposeful with it or not. Don't allow your attention to be on autopilot, taken over by whatever comes your way. Choose where and how you invest it.

Throughout your day take notice of where your attention is. Is it being given over to productive thoughts of creativity, appreciation, and contribution? Or is it being given over to disappointment, obstacles, and complaining?

Think of your attention like any other resource. Use it wisely. Let your attention be an investment, not a liability. Know that whatever you put your attention on will grow. You know the saying, "Give him an inch, he'll take a mile." That is what happens with our attention, so make sure you are spending it on an area you want to see grow. Know this; whatever you choose to focus on will expand.

When you recognize that your attention has been given over to unproductive things, such as complaining, worry, gossip, or fear, simply shift your attention onto whatever it is that you would like more of, love, joy, gratitude, peace, contribution, creativity, harmony, generosity, fun, and happiness.

Plan ahead. Start your day out on the right track by choosing to be purposeful in what you give your attention to and experience a great sense of empowerment and improved results. Do it now, write down what you are willing to give your attention to today and like a magnet, watch how your attention will be drawn to those things you wrote down.

# My Journal

_____

_____

_____

_____

_____

_____

_____

_____

_____

_____

_____

_____

_____

_____

_____

_____

_____

_____

*See the purpose in your storm.*

# 6. PURPOSE

*"Every problem has in it the seeds of its own solution. If you don't have any problems, you don't get any seeds." ~ Norman Vincent Peale*

Every storm has a purpose. Storms come to our lives to test us, reveal what is within, and produce strength. We have all been through difficult times and the more turbulent the storm, the more strength and beauty it will produce in you.

During one of the most difficult times of my life, I surely felt like I was in the middle of a storm. I was fearful and disoriented with doubts, confusion, and I felt completely alone. At first I spent great efforts trying to figure out my storm. I tried relentlessly to conquer it. I strived and strained to get rid of it. I exhausted my mind composing plans that only failed to make it go away. Despite my efforts to make my storm dissipate, I made no progress.

When I recognized that I had depleted my will and my efforts, I resolved to embrace the storm for what it was. It was there for a purpose and that purpose was good. It was there to produce greatness in me. Just like palm trees, my storm had come to break my ground and deepen my roots.

When I finally made peace with my storm and accepted the uncertainty, I experienced a change on the inside, calming me. Though nothing had changed on the outside, nor did it for quite a while after. But the change on the inside created in me a new focus, one of peace, appreciation and trust. My inner strength was revealed and I am now so grateful for that time in my life. It revealed to me who I really am.

Whatever storm you may be in, just know that it is there for a reason and that reason is good. Don't resist it. Don't run away from it. Let the storm run its course and reveal to you new insights. Allow the storm to do its work inside and you will be delighted at what shows up outside. Just know that the storm will pass and you will be stronger than before.

# My Journal

_____

_____

_____

_____

_____

_____

_____

_____

_____

_____

_____

_____

_____

_____

_____

_____

_____

_____

# 7. SURRENDER

*"God, grant me the serenity to accept the things I cannot change, the courage to change the things I can, and wisdom to know the difference."* ~ *Reinhold Niebuhr*

Would you like more peace, joy, and happiness in your life? Well, if you do, you can create more of it through surrender, acceptance and by simply letting things go. Stress on the other hand, will rob or dilute our ability to enjoy life.

Where does stress come from? The main cause of stress is resistance to that which is out of our hands. You may be able to recognize resistance on a vast scale and in a variety of areas. Resistance appears in situations as simple as not getting your parking spot, or as complex as the loss of a loved one. Any situation or circumstance that we resist creates stress.

Take a few minutes now to recognize and identify any areas that may be causing you stress. Take inventory of where your mental, physical, and spiritual energy is going.

1. Write down the things/people/events that are creating stress for you.

2. Next to each item write, "Yes" if you can do something about it or, "No" if it is out of your hands.

3. For the items you wrote "Yes" next to, write down what action you choose to take to resolve it and when you will complete it by. Pull out your calendar and book the appointment time that you will take care of it.

4. For the items that are out of your control, write down the method you will use to LET IT GO.

The method may be a matter of you praying or meditating to release the burden. It may be that you write in your journal. It may be you simply saying, "I let this go" out loud. Sometimes, just identifying it and choosing to let it go is all it takes.

Choose now to **LET GO of the things that are out of your control.** Take action on the things that are within your control and enjoy the extra energy you have from doing so.

# My Journal

_____

_____

_____

_____

_____

_____

_____

_____

_____

_____

_____

_____

_____

_____

_____

_____

Enjoy this present moment now.

# 8. PRESENCE

*"The supreme value is not the future but the present. Whoever builds a house for future happiness builds a prison for the present."* ~ *Octavio Paz*

One wet fall morning my cousin Sara and I were running along Folsom Lake. She asked me if I lived in the past, present or the future. I knew my answer immediately. My thoughts were consumed with the future. Her question really got my attention. In answering her, I recognized what had been robbing my joy. The solution was clear. Live in the present. Let go of the past and do not be concerned with the future.

The problem with spending our thoughts on the past or the future is that we are trading something that doesn't exist for what does exist. We cannot change our past and there is no guarantee we will have a future, but what we can be certain of, is that we have this moment. Worry is the biggest culprit in stealing our present moment. Think of some of the biggest worries most of us struggle with – worries about money. Even if you are going bankrupt, you rob yourself of the present reality when you get stuck on what will happen in the future.

So what would it take to enjoy this moment? It is as simple as a decision. When we decide to be present we ignite our awareness and it automatically brings us present. Being present causes sadness, longing, and regret to vanish. Being present provides space for peace, joy, appreciation, and happiness. I encourage you to enjoy your life by being present with this moment and appreciate that you have it.

Enjoy this moment right now. Use your 5 senses. Write down what you hear, see, taste, feel, and smell. Take a few deep breaths and take in your surroundings. You are probably starting to feel some appreciation come to you. Write down the things you appreciate. There, you are present in this moment. You can do this any time you feel yourself go into your past or considering your future. Make being present a daily habit and enjoy all that it creates for you.

# My Journal

_____

_____

_____

_____

_____

_____

_____

_____

_____

_____

_____

_____

_____

_____

_____

_____

*Find the choice
in every situation.*

# 9. CHOICE

*"I am the greatest, I said that even before I knew I was." ~ Muhammad Ali*

We cannot control the hand that is dealt to us. However, we can choose how we play that hand. Life is full of choices, but it is up to us to see that we have a choice and then to make a choice. Too often we don't view life as a sea of choices. Instead we see it from a place of default, having to make due with what we have and settle with where we are.

One area I ask that you consider today is the choice of who you are and who you are becoming. It really doesn't matter where you started or what you have done. Some are given a great start with every resource and opportunity; others start out with the world working against them. Either group could go either way- into a fulfilled and purposeful life or into disappointment and misery. The ONLY difference is what they choose.

So, what do you choose for your life and your future? It is NEVER, and I mean NEVER, too late to shift your life course. Don't waste a thought reflecting on past mistakes or misfortunes. Instead use that energy into creating your future. Just making a choice and creating a vision for who you are becoming is enough to fuel you to have the life you always wanted. If you were the author of your own life's story, what would you write next? Where are you going? Who will you become? How does it end? It truly is up to you

Start right now. Take a few minutes to author your story. Spend some time every day to continue creating your book. You can choose where you are going and what you will become. If you don't author it, default will.

# My Journal

_____

_____

_____

_____

_____

_____

_____

_____

_____

_____

_____

_____

_____

_____

_____

_____

_____

*Turn any problem around
through serving, giving, & sharing.*

# 10. SHIFT IT

*"You can have everything you want in life, if you help enough other people get what they want"* ~ *Zig Ziglar*

Do you have a specific challenge in your life that is bugging you? How much time and energy is your current challenge costing you? We all have our own set of struggles and disappointments. That is life. The fact is…WHAT WE FOCUS ON EXPANDS. Therefore, when we have a problem, the more we worry about it, the heavier the burden it becomes.

Would you like to shift that burden and get the weight of it off of your shoulders? It can easily be done. Simply shift your attention off of your problems and on to a more productive focus. The more productive focus would be, "WHO CAN I HELP TODAY?"

Despite the current challenges you are facing, you are always capable of helping someone else. My dad has always told me, "There's always gonna be someone who has more than you, but there's also always someone else who has less." Which of the two sides do you chose to focus on? You see it doesn't matter how low you feel or how down you are. If you stop and look around, you will find someone who could use your help. By stopping and helping that other person, you will experience the shift in your cares and concerns. Through serving and helping others we gain joy, purpose, and prosperity. The very key needed to unlock your breakthrough can be found through serving and helping others.

I encourage you today to pause your busy life and find at least one person and one way to help someone. Below are some ideas:

- Send a note card of encouragement or appreciation to a co-worker, family member, or neighbor.

- Anonymously send flowers to someone who could use some color in their day.

- Make a meal for a family or elderly neighbor.

- Mow a lawn for a neighbor.

- Give something you don't use away, instead of selling it.

- Volunteer an afternoon at a shelter or non-profit.

- Go to a park and pick up trash.

Every day there are so many opportunities to help others. Be on the look out and seize every opportunity, then watch the levels of joy and prosperity in your life rise.

# My Journal

_____

_____

_____

_____

_____

_____

_____

_____

_____

_____

_____

_____

_____

_____

_____

_____

_____

_____

_____

*Look inside instead of outside
to find your answers.*

# 11. RESOURCEFULNESS

*"He who knows he has enough is rich." ~ Tao Te Ching*

**Lack of money isn't real.** That's a pretty bold statement to grasp, especially when a financial hardship is present. What I mean by that statement is that thinking and believing we don't have enough money limits us tremendously. The root belief here is, "I need money for…" Is money really the only means to being able to have or do? That way of thinking creates a very narrow reality and shuts down possibilities. It ultimately stops us from doing what we can. The truth is there are endless possibilities when we are open to seeing them and when we let go of the belief that we don't have enough.

The belief that we don't have enough money is a conditioned way of thinking that says we need something outside of ourselves to obtain what we want. It is the ultimate marketing plan causing us to need or want more.

Have you ever thought, "Once I have more money, I'll be able to relax," or "Once I have enough money, I'll visit another country," or "Once I have more money, I'll be more generous," or "Once I have enough money I'll have more fun"?

When you find yourself thinking those thoughts, STOP. Ask yourself, "What can I do now, with what I have and who I am now?" If you are willing to let go of the belief that you need more, you will tap into a creative resource that is full of possibilities. You will connect with others that will want to help and support you. You will have what you desire and more will flow into your life.

When I was going through one of my worst financial times, I had no steady income. I was a single mom, selling real estate and I was broke. I had depleted my little 401k to ensure I could pay for my rent, gas and groceries. I had always wanted a large kitchen table to have family over for meals, and clearly now wasn't the time for me to spend money on something like that. One day, I was on a listing appointment and the couple I was meeting with were divorcing and downsizing. In conversation I had briefly complimented their beautiful table. We went on with the paperwork and off I left. The next day I got a call from the woman, saying that she and her husband wanted to give me their table. Oh, my goodness! I was so happy! This table was exactly what I had imaged buying one day. It was dark wood. The design was very simple, elegant and rustic. I knew right there that I was going to be ok. My financial struggles would not limit me from having and doing what I wanted. I knew there were endless possibilities of HOW I would have the life of my dreams. I no longer looked at money as the only means to obtaining my heart's desires.

So, where are you today? What are you believing is possible or impossible based on your current resources? STOP believing you need something outside of yourself to obtain what you desire. You already have everything you need. Allow your resourcefulness and creativity to produce what you want.

# My Journal

*Abundance is a choice.*

# 12. ABUNDANCE

*"Abundance is not something we acquire. It is something we tune into." ~ Wayne Dyer*

Abundance is a mindset. It is not simply what we have. It is how we see. With an abundant mindset we see and feel that we have more than enough, regardless of our external circumstances. That outlook creates freedom, void of worry and stress. It is a place of knowing that all needs are met. Abundant thinking sees overflow and creates a natural sense of generosity.

With scarcity on the other hand, there is a feeling of lack, need, want, and not enough. Scarcity creates a "barely get by, survival" mentality. A scarcity mindset will cause you to want to hold on to things. It is difficult to share with emotions of scarcity because of the concern for oneself. Thoughts of, "It's mine. I need." are present. A key indicator of scarcity is fear; fear that someone or something will take what you have or that you will loose it.

Abundance cannot be present in scarcity and scarcity cannot be present in abundance, so, which would you prefer, abundance or scarcity? I'm guessing you are like me and prefer abundance. So, how do we create an abundant mindset, when lack is present? Well, it is a choice. Make the decision to develop a mindset of abundance and begin to take action from that place of abundance. From there, you will create more than enough. You will attract more than enough.

I have experienced this in an extremely challenging area, with my children. Since my divorce, I have had to "share" my children. In the beginning I was overwhelmed with emotions of scarcity, wanting them every chance I could. I battled thoughts and emotions of not having enough time with them and not having enough influence on them. I battled scarcity in just about every area you could imagine. This scarcity consumed me. I eventually became exhausted from my scarcity mindset and surrendered to abundance. That choice eventually created the abundance that I longed for.

You can develop the abundance you long for, in whatever area you may be experiencing scarcity in, by simply choosing. Decide today to see your situation with abundance, more than enough time, more than enough money, more than enough attention, more than enough love. Watch your mindset and actions create abundance and joy.

# My Journal

*Recharge your battery with energy infusers.*

# 13. ENERGY

*"The higher your energy level, the more efficient your body the more efficient your body, the better you feel and the more you will use your talent to produce outstanding results." ~ Tony Robbins*

When I got my first smart phone, one of my biggest complaints was that the battery would drain too quickly. Before noon I had to recharge it. What I learned is that certain applications consumed more battery life than others. Once I figured that out, I was more purposeful with how I used my phone and my battery would easily last all day. This is no different than our own lives.

Every day, we start out with a certain amount of energy- physical, mental and emotional, and it is up to us to ensure we have ample energy for our entire day. So, how do we plan, prepare and maintain plenty of energy for the day? One way is to know what our energy drainers and our energy infusers are. We make hundreds of choices each day that either drain our energy or recharge it. Our choices with food, choices with our thoughts, choices with our actions, and choices of who we hang around with, are all either increasing or decreasing our energy.

One thing I have recently done to help keep my energy re-charging was to create an energy infuser list. I listed things and people that are fun or make me feel good. The things that are fun were pretty obvious, but the things that make me feel good required a little more thought. Because there are things that may not feel good at the time, but end up re-energizing me afterward, like going for a run, eating a salad, cleaning out my car, going to bed early, etc.

What and who are your energy infusers? Keep a running list of who and what re-charge you and then make sure that you are putting energy infusers on your calendar. Delete or eliminate as many energy drainers as possible. Watch how your days are more productive, enjoyable and fulfilling!

# My Journal

_____

_____

_____

_____

_____

_____

_____

_____

_____

_____

_____

_____

_____

_____

_____

_____

_____

_____

Celebrate failure as a gift
in helping you grow.

# 14. GROW

*"There are no failures-just experiences and your reaction to them."* ~ *Tom Krause*

What is failure? Some synonyms of failure are breakdown, stoppage, malfunction, crash, and collapse. Have you experienced a collapse in a relationship? A stoppage in finances? Any malfunction with your plans? A crash in your efforts? A breakdown in communication?

If you can answer yes to any of those questions, you can celebrate. Those malfunctions are opportunities for you to grow and to learn. So, how do we grow from a failure? Well, the questions we ask ourselves immediately following any failure will determine whether or not we learn. Asking questions that lead to understanding create growth. Asking questions that lead to searching for someone or something to blame prohibit growth. When we blame others for our failures we compromise the possibility to learn and grow from those experiences.

Have you ever found yourself dealing with the same failure over and over? If so, you can, again, celebrate. You see, when the same problem shows up again and again, it is providing you with as many opportunities necessary for you to learn and grow in that area. If the same failure keeps showing up, see it as extra chances to work through that problem. Don't dwell on the failures. Instead see each failure as a highly valuable learning experience that can provide you a treasure of wisdom and understanding.

Below are some great questions you can ask yourself to create a learning experience from any failure:

- What lessons have I learned from this situation?
- What can I be grateful for from this experience?
- What can I do to turn this failure into a success?
- Where do I go from here?
- Who else has failed in this way before, and how can that person (or their experience) help me?

- How can my experience help others someday to keep from failing in this area?
- What were some of the contributing factors to this failure?
- Where did I succeed as well as fail?

I encourage you today- use every single failure as an opportunity to grow and learn. Use the questions above to grow from your most recent failure and enjoy the growth it will create for you.

# My Journal

*Let enthusiasm and hope create your path to abundance.*

# 15. ENTHUSIASM

*"Empty pockets never held anyone back. Only empty heads and empty hearts can do that." ~ Norman Vincent Peale.*

During a financially challenging time, I learned a great lesson about enthusiasm and hope. I wrote about my experience and several years after that time, I was thumbing through an old journal and came across what I had written. I thought about re-writing my experience, but felt it would take away from it, so I'll keep my expressions intact and share with you exactly what I wrote.

*"So, I would say in the past year or so, I have had some tough times financially. I was at my cute little apartment yesterday taking care of my little angel, Jayden. He had surgery that morning when I heard a knock at the door. I went to open it and it was the PG&E man. I have been behind on my PG&E since December (Christmas lights bill). I pay $100 every month, but apparently that wasn't enough to stop PG&E from shutting off my service. He was gracious enough to allow me to call in and make a payment over the phone, which I did right then and prevented it from being shut off. As he was leaving, we were casually talking. After some humorous conversations with Jayden and myself, we got to talking about the economy and real estate. When he found out I was selling real estate, he began in on how horrible it is for realtors making such small commissions, etc. I responded with my typical excitement and enthusiasm about the business and my outlook was made clear to him. We started talking about the various opportunities in the current market and what was working. As it turns out, he owns dozens of rentals and just bought another. He is looking now for a fourplex! The more we got to talking he ended up sharing his complimentary discernment of my abilities and gave me his info for me to look for a property for him.*

*Long story short, when you develop a genuinely positive outlook, it will shine. It will shine especially bright during the dark times and as crazy as it sounds- the man that came to shut off my PG&E, is now my client. Despite my current financial challenge it is pretty apparent that it is only a temporary challenge and what I like to think of as a training period."*

Even today, when I read what I wrote, I can remember the way I felt during that time and on that day. I was under much more than financial pressure. My entire life was in upheaval, going through a divorce, uncertain about all I thought I had and knew. My mind and emotions flooded daily with fears, doubts and worries. I also remember this vein of hope, optimism and enthusiasm that kept me alive, kept me moving forward and that is what the PG&E man saw and felt from me. I encourage you today to find your enthusiasm. Find your hope in every situation. You have it. Tap into it and let it flow out of you. Your enthusiasm will create your path from your challenge to your success.

I encourage you this week; just know, whatever you are facing, it is temporary. It will pass. You can have enthusiasm and hope in every difficult situation.

# My Journal

*Find the fun in EVERY
disappointment or obstacle.*

# 16. THE PERFECT GAME

*"Make a game of finding something positive in every situation. 95% of your emotions are determined by how you interpret events to yourself." ~ Brian Tracy.*

Our lives would drastically improve if we were to start playing The "Perfect" Game, every day all day. The "Perfect" Game works like this…any time something goes wrong — being late to work, forgotten homework, pay cut, or a fight with a friend — no matter what it is- say to yourself, "That's perfect." Then think of all the reasons it is perfect. The more challenging the obstacle, the more creative you will become in finding a reason why it's perfect.

It may be a bit of a challenge, when you first start this game, to come up with reasons it's perfect that you ripped a hole in a new pair of pants, or you got a pay-cut. But if you are willing to play, you will find reasons. And as you develop the habit of playing this game, your thought process will begin to change. It will become easier and easier to see why disappointments and delays are perfect. You will be able to see how all things work to your benefit. It will become your natural thought process and that is where the real beauty shows up. That is when your creativity will produce endless possibilities.

You can play this game with your kids, grandkids, nieces, nephews, co-workers and neighbors. We have a lot of fun hearing the silly reasons my kids come up with. We are creating a culture of creativity in our world and I encourage you to do the same in yours! Try it out today and this week. If something doesn't work out as planned or if a disappointment pops up, just remember to say to yourself, "It's perfect!" and begin to think of the reasons why everything *will* work out in your favor.

# My Journal

_____

_____

_____

_____

_____

_____

_____

_____

_____

_____

_____

_____

_____

_____

_____

_____

*Take a moment to decide what you want for this moment and this day.*

# 17. INTENTION

*"Quality is never an accident; it is always the result of high intention, sincere effort, intelligent direction and skillful execution; it represents the wise choice of many alternatives."* ~ William A. Foster

Our current environment and culture of technology, accessibility and speed has undoubtedly created a lifestyle of busyness. Busyness often forfeits intention. And intention is exactly what we need to have enjoyment and fulfillment in our lives. One definition for the word intention is, "an aim, objective or the quality of purposefulness." Based on those definitions, can you see how important having intention is? Without intention, we are left to default, and able to be tossed in the wind.

Having intention and focus in just about any situation can dramatically improve your quality of life. I can recall one of my first experiences of noticing how intention makes a difference. I had lunch plans with three friends from work. On the way to the lunch, I put some thought into what I wanted the lunch to be like. I thought about how I would like to have great conversations with my friends and learn more about each of them. Our lunch accomplished those intentions. I had enriching conversations and discovered new things about each person.

Would I have had such enriching conversations, without the intention? Maybe...maybe not. It's uncertain. Without the intention, it would have been left up to luck and chance.

Try it for yourself. Be intentional about what you want out of your daily routines, your meetings, your conversations or any event going on in your life. Our lives are precious. Time goes by with or without intention, so why not try to get the most out of our lives? I encourage you today, set your mind on what you want to accomplish, and on what you want to have. Intend on having great conversations. Intend on having a steady sense of peace or joy. Intend on achieving the success you desire. See what happens when you live with intention. You will be pleasantly surprised.

# My Journal

*Look for the
pathways to flow.*

# 18. FLOW

*"Be content with what you have, rejoice in the way things are. When you realize there is nothing lacking, the whole world belongs to you." ~ Lao Tzu*

Finding your flow is as simple as knowing what you want and where you are going, while embracing everything that disrupts your plans, as ingredients to your success. Flow is simple but not easy. Finding this flow requires surrender, flexibility, creativity and appreciation. We must surrender the need to control.

In the book *Power vs. Force*, author David Hawkins extensively explores this truth. He explains the contrast of forcing something versus allowing. Force and domination may appear to have power, but they are actually rooted in fear and the need to control. There is no power in fear and in fact, the need for control is imprisoning. On the contrary, when we are free from force and in a prosperous flow, we are free from fear and free from the need to control. We are taking actions rooted from faith, hope, love, and abundance.

Where in your world are you experiencing struggle, strain or stress? Where are you feeling weary, due to effort and over-exertion? When these emotions are present, you can be sure there is some domination at work, fighting against what is and trying to force what you want into existence. When you recognize this, you can choose to release that force. Let go of the fear and step into the flow of acceptance. That is true power.

When I find myself in that place of force and domination, I pause and give myself some space to allow clarity. I make a choice to stop resisting what is. From that space of allowance, I can see options and pathways. I am in peace and ease and almost immediately, I can take action from a place of flow.

Don't miss opportunities by trying to force your desires into existence. Instead choose surrender, appreciation, and enjoy the flow in your life.

# My Journal

_____

_____

_____

_____

_____

_____

_____

_____

_____

_____

_____

_____

_____

_____

_____

*Recognize irritations as a signal
for growth and change.*

# 19. SIGNALS

*"If you don't like something, change it. If you can't change it, change your attitude."* ~ Maya Angelo

When something is uncomfortable or displeasing, we generally try to make it go away. When we have a headache, we take an aspirin, instead of asking, "What is my body signaling?" Discomfort and irritation are actually signals. They're flashing yellow signs that say, "Slow down. Pay attention. Something is going on." A headache can be provoked by thirst, so if we take an aspirin and make the headache go away, the dehydration is still there. The signal is just covered.

One of the emotions I avoid is irritation. I don't like irritation. It is annoying and makes me cranky. In recent days, I had found myself having an increased level of irritation. I tried all my positive attitude tricks, like reading inspiring books, writing affirmations, listening to uplifting music, but the irritation just wouldn't go away. I found myself being snappy with my family and those around me. Since none of my efforts seemed to be working, I decided to look up the word irritation. Some of the synonyms for irritation were motivation, stimulus, and provocation.

Reading that completely shifted my perspective on this irritation and why it was present in my life. I began looking at this irritation as a tool to help me grow, a tool to provoke me into action. I was then able to recognize that the irritation was created from my stagnancy, being in my comfort zone too long. It was time for change, time for growth, and time for me to get out of my cozy little comfort bed and step into my greatness. Thank God I recognized what my irritation was signaling instead of covering it up with entertainment or avoidance.

Where do you have irritation in your life? Why is that irritation there? What is it signaling for you? It may be telling you to break the status quo and challenge yourself. It may be telling you to stretch, get out of your comfort zone. When you experience irritation, be open to see that it is there to produce greatness and growth in your life. Get up, get going and let irritation motivate you to take action and provoke growth.

# My Journal

_____

_____

_____

_____

_____

_____

_____

_____

_____

_____

_____

_____

_____

_____

_____

_____

_____

_____

*Align your outer life with your inner life.*

# 20. ALIGNMENT

*"The indispensable first step to getting the things you want out of life is this: decide what you want." ~ Ben Stein*

We all have an outer life and an inner life. The outer life is our public life that everyone else can see, composed of our behaviors and our results. We often focus on our outer life, with everyone else. Our inner life is unseen and made up of our thoughts, our attitudes and our motives. To be in alignment, we must connect our outer life with our inner life and doing that simply takes a little attention.

Too often we get busy rushing here and there, meeting others' expectations, unaware of what our inner life is telling us. Have you ever committed to attend an event and after you were there, realized that you really didn't want to be there in the first place? This is a perfect example of our outer life being disconnected with our inner life. We get out of alignment when this happens. When we are out of alignment, we cannot live in efficiency and ease.

To create alignment, we must listen to our inner life or our inner voice and then take action. Our inner voice may be telling us to calm down, relax, and be still. It may be telling us to go for it, make a change, but how will we know what it is saying if we are not listening? Too often we look outside of ourselves for direction and answers. We look at the circumstances in our outer life to make those logical decisions. But if we were to slow down and listen to our inner voice, then take action, we would be in alignment and able to have efficiency, and ease.

Where do you feel out of alignment? Where is there a disconnect? If you are experiencing a disconnect, stop, slow down and listen inward, listening for guidance and clarity. It is when we line up our outer life with our inner life that we get into a prosperous flow. Our relationships have more harmony, the productivity in our work increases, and our happiness is high. Align your outer life with your inner life today.

# My Journal

*Recognize the benefits
in every experience.*

# 21. THINGS HAPPEN FOR US

*"There is no security in this life. There is only opportunity." ~ Douglas MacArthur*

Sometimes things happen in our lives that are beyond our control. Though we may never understand why difficulties arise, we can choose to believe, they occur for our good. Job loss, heartbreak, loosing our wallet, whatever the problem is, we have the option in how we respond. Responding with, "Why is this happening to me? It's not fair" are thoughts that deepen the disappointment. If rather, we choose to believe, that things happen for us, instead of to us, it repositions us in a place of progress.

When my youngest brother started high school, my mom decided it was time for her to go after her lifelong dream of being a teacher. Going back to school after 20 years was really challenging, but she succeeded and got her teaching credentials. Right about that time, the economy and education system went down. The first few years after her graduation, she couldn't get a job and took whatever sub days were offered her.

She finally got a job, but at the end of the year got a pink slip. Every year following was the same story. She would get hired at a new school, new grade level, get established, then pink slip, and this repeated for several years.

The first few years, I was so angry. I was so frustrated for my mom, seeing what hard work she had done to get her credentials. I was thinking, "This isn't fair. Why is this happening to her? My mom has done nothing for herself all these years and when she finally has the time to do what she wants, she can't get anywhere!"  Well, what I witnessed from my mom is that, she didn't stay in that, "Why is this happening to me?" mentality. She just made the best of her options. She made the most out of her situation and doors have continued to open. Her positive outlook further developed great flexibility, patience, faith and tenacity in her. She got comfortable being uncomfortable. She demonstrated this lesson that things don't happen to us, they happen for us.

So, how do you respond to difficulty and disappointment? Do you ask why or do you choose to believe it is working for your good? If you choose to believe it is happening for you, then no challenge, disappointment or obstacle will defeat you. You will be able to bounce back from anything. And when that difficult time has passed, your experience will give hope and encouragement to others. Keep heart during any challenge. Know that the difficulty will pass and will produce greatness in your life!

# My Journal

*Where there's a will,*
*there's a way.*

# 22. PIG STORY

*"If you can dream it, you can do it." ~ Walt Disney*

When I was in 11$^{th}$ grade I decided I wanted to raise a pig for the county fair. I went to Atwater High, in an agricultural town and always had an interest, but didn't have the money or the space. My best friend, Kilie was raising her first pig at her papa's house in the country and I wanted to as well. I told my parents what I wanted to do and they said I could. Only catch, I needed to come up with the money and find a place to raise it. I asked Papa if he would be willing to allow me to use his property and if he would front me the money for food and supplies. I would repay him once I sold the pig at auction. He said yes.

I had another hurdle to overcome. How was I going to buy the pig?

It was over $200 and I only had a week to get the money. I tried to think of who I could borrow the money from, but had no promising prospects.  As I was walking home from school one day, an idea took me on a little detour to County Bank. I walked into the bank and got in line like any other customer. When the teller asked, "How can I help you?" I responded, "Who makes the decisions here?" I didn't know to ask for the branch manager.

Caught by surprise, she walked me over to the branch manager and as I walked into his office, I suddenly got nervous, realizing I had no idea what I was doing or what I was to say. But since I had the manager's time and attention, I described my situation and determination to raise a pig for the fair. I built my case as a "qualified borrower," having a 4.0 and a plan for re-payment. I can still see his facial expressions, clearly revealing his desire to help me. He asked me to provide a copy of my report card, a referral letter from one of my teachers and written consent from my parents. By the next day, I signed an unsecured promissory note for $240 and I had my money to buy my pig.

I was so happy to pick out my pig and every day afterschool I would go to feed him and clean up his pin and the closer the fair came I began to hear the other students talking about "their buyers." As I probed to find out what they meant by "buyers" I learned that most of the kids' parents had connections and arrangements for who would be buying their pig. My heart sank and for the first time feared the possibility of not being able to pay back my debts to Papa and to the bank.

As I walked home heavy hearted, my wheels were spinning, "Who was going to buy my pig?" And just about the time I was walking by Lucky (our local grocery store) I thought, "Meat department!" So, I walked in, went straight to customer service and asked who was in charge of the meat department. They ended up connecting me with the store manager, Roy Torres. As I began to explain my dilemma and need for a buyer, I saw Roy's eyes light up and I could see he too wanted to help me. He assured me that my pig would be purchased at auction.

When the day of the auction arrived, I saw Roy out in the stands and my heart was overjoyed when he won the bid and purchased my pig. I not only sold my pig and paid back my debts, but also earned a few extra bucks for my pocket. The next year I repeated the entire event, with the help of the bank and Roy and successfully sold my 2nd pig. It was the 2nd year that I realized Lucky meat department didn't buy my pig. Roy did and it brings tears of appreciation to my eyes, even today.

When I find myself feeling stuck, like my hands are tied, I remember back to my pig story and how determined I was to accomplish my heart's desire. I choose to live with that same belief, determination and zeal. Whatever you want for your life, you can have. You just gotta take a step at a time. You are creative, resourceful and able to accomplish anything you want!

# My Journal

_____

_____

_____

_____

_____

_____

_____

_____

_____

_____

_____

_____

_____

_____

_____

_____

_____

*Allow disappointment to produce character and strength.*

# 23. PREVAIL

*"When you get into a tight place and everything goes against you, till it seems as though you could not hold on a minute longer, never give up then, for that is just the place and time that the tide will turn." ~ Harriet Beecher Stowe*

The way to prevail from life's disappointments is to plan and prepare to prevail.

Disappointment and failure have visited us all, at one time or another. We all know we should "look on the bright side." But when we are in the middle of a disappointment, the last thing we feel like doing is looking on the bright side. So, how then, can we? I say, "Have a plan in place for how you respond to disappointments."

Be prepared for disappointments by developing and maintaining a strong positive outlook. When disappointment shows up in my life, the first thing I do, is mentally disconnect from the outcome. I embrace worst-case scenario and look for the good. Often times the only good I can entertain is the value in the learning of a lesson. I think of it like an award or like earning a degree in the school of hard knocks. I just think, well, I'll never do that again. Or, wow, what a small price to pay for a priceless lesson. I have found that if I plan ahead of time to see the learning lesson with each disappointment or with each "failure" I am able to get over it quicker.

I have made many mistakes, some much worse than others, and the only thing that keeps regret and disappointment from paralyzing me and stifling my growth is that I choose to let it go and be grateful for the learning lesson. Disappointment and failure will continue to try to creep in, so be prepared with an outlook of appreciation for the wisdom gained in every situation. Without disappointment or failure, we wouldn't be able to experience the confidence and strength that is produced when we prevail.

# My Journal

_____

_____

_____

_____

_____

_____

_____

_____

_____

_____

_____

_____

_____

_____

_____

_____

_____

*Who you are remains.*

# 24. ESSENCE

*"The sculptor produces the beautiful statue by chipping away such parts of the marble block as are not needed- it is a process of elimination."* ~ *Elbert Hubbard*

Too often we look at what is on the outside as a determiner of what is on the inside. You have heard the saying, "Don't judge a book by its cover." Yet we do it all the time. Not only do we do this with others, but we also do it with ourselves. We focus on our need to loose more weight (external), earn more income (external), or break bad habits (external). I spent most of my life judging myself and focusing on the external things, what I was doing and what I had accomplished. It wasn't until my external world collapsed that I was able to see what was true, which is who I am, my heart, my essence. Who we are does not change. It is our external shells that change. When we find and maintain our essence, we are unshakable.

At the beginning of 2008, my world began unraveling and it unraveled quickly. I lost just about everything I thought I had. I was very scared because I had exhausted my mental, emotional and spiritual abilities trying to hold onto my marriage, my finances, and my "picture perfect" life that I had worked so hard to build. The more I tried to fix my situation, the worse it got. It was like I was drowning and trying to save myself from drowning, which only ensured my death. I finally got smart and just STOPPED, stopped trying. I just got still. I surrendered.

In my stillness, I found a great loss heavy on my heart. My effort to fix my situation had been covering the grief and now that I was no longer trying to fix my situation, the grief was surfacing. I made new attempts to find comfort, but every attempt proved unsuccessful, so again, all I could do was be still. And when I was still for long enough, I was finally able to see what was left: my essence, who I am. Who I am can never be taken or broken and it is beautiful.

In finding my essence, I knew I had everything I needed all along. My external world had to be broken down and shed for me to see whom I was. For the first time in my life I was in a position to enjoy my riches. It was from this place that I was able to pick myself up, crawl out of my deep, dark, hole and take one step at a time to rebuild my life. I now look back at that painful time with great appreciation. It has given me the priceless gift of shedding my life of all that was not real. I am now able to live in a state of knowing who I am.

The weaker we feel, the greater the work. In my weakness state, my strength was tested and revealed and I like what has surfaced in the shedding away. Whatever area you experience weakness, just know that it is there to reveal your strength. Who you are is greater than any external circumstance. Allow your essence to be revealed and accept your unchangeable beauty.

# My Journal

_____

_____

_____

_____

_____

_____

_____

_____

_____

_____

_____

_____

_____

_____

_____

_____

_____

_____

*Create and maintain balance.*

# 25. BALANCE

*"The willingness to accept responsibility for one's own life is the source from which self-respect springs."* ~ Joan Didion

What is the importance of balance? What does it take for you to have balance? What happens when you get out of balance? These are all very important questions for you to consider when making commitments. We all have an "oops factor." An oops factor is the point we get to from doing too much where we crash and burn. Sometimes it shows up in our health when our body demands some down time, to recoup and get back in balance. If you know your limits ahead of time, you will be able to maintain balance without a crash and burn.

Balance is important for stability and progress. How well can you perform when you are out of balance? When I am out of balance, I find myself very agitated and less tolerable of irritating things. When I am out of balance, I am certainly not content. Unfortunately, sometimes it takes getting a little out of balance to recognize I need to get myself back in balance.

I remember having a conversation with a friend about balance. I set a goal to obtain balance and his response shifted my perspective. His response was that balance isn't real; it's an illusion. Basically, balance isn't something we can go buy or go get, then check it off our list and be done with it. When we achieve balance, we must maintain it with continual counterbalancing. Look at a dancer or a gymnast. When a dancer holds a pose, you will hear the viewers say, "ahhh, look at that perfect balance." But if you were to look closely, you would see all the muscles in her body continually counter balancing, providing the appearance that she is in balance.

The same is true in our lives. We must know what our limits are in keeping our lives in balance and then make sure to keep up with the counter balancing. As life changes, our limits will adjust and to maintain balance, we too must adjust. Take a quick inventory of how balanced you are right now. Make a list of all the areas that are important to you, and then rate them. Which areas received a low rating, pulling you out of balance and what would it take to get you back in balance? A lot of time it isn't a major change that is necessary. It may be a minor adjustment like a 15-minute walk in the morning or cutting back on dessert a few nights a week. You can create and maintain balance through keeping an eye on your counter balancing. Tackle one area today and experience the efficiency being in balance creates.

# My Journal

_____

_____

_____

_____

_____

_____

_____

_____

_____

_____

_____

_____

_____

_____

_____

_____

*Find simplicity. Find freedom.*

# 26. SIMPLICITY

*"Any intelligent fool can make things bigger, more complex, and more violent. It takes a touch of genius – and a lot of courage – to move in the opposite direction." ~ E. F. Schumacker*

Keep life simple. It doesn't have to be complicated. We make it complicated. Complication makes things hard. Simplicity makes things easy. Keeping it simple is a way of life. Keeping it simple is a mindset we can choose. Don't buy the lie that you cannot focus. Being distracted and given over to spontaneity is just a conditioned reflex. If we are able to develop the ability to be distracted, we are able to develop the ability to be focused. Simplicity creates the environment for focus, purpose and enjoyment.

Feeling overwhelmed disappears instantly in the presence of simplicity. Prioritizing and focusing is easy in simplicity. Simplicity allows options to be seen very clearly.

What would it take for you to create more simplicity in your life? One of the greatest steps towards simplicity is elimination. There are certain things we can simply eliminate to create the space for simplicity. I love the quote below.

*"A man must be able to cut a knot, for everything cannot be untied; he must know how to disengage what is essential from the detail in which it is enwrapped, for everything cannot be equally considered; in a word, he must be able to simplify his duties, his business and his life." ~ Henri Frederic Amiel*

After reading that quote, what comes to mind for you? What knots are you willing to cut, so that you can be freed up for a life of purpose and enjoyment? Take note, anytime you find yourself overwhelmed, cut away any unnecessary considerations, so that simplicity and freedom can surface. Do it today- find simplicity and you will find freedom and ease.

# My Journal

*Use obstacles to create prosperity.*

# 27. LEMONADE

*"If your house is on fire, warm yourself by it." ~ Spanish Proverb*

*"The most important thing in life is not to capitalize on your gains. Any fool can do that. The really important thing is to profit from your losses. That requires intelligence; and it makes the difference between a man of sense and a fool." ~ William Bolitho*

Every experience we have is an ingredient for success. Looking at problems as opportunities is the perfect environment for creativity to be birthed. Have you ever found yourself exhausted from efforts of eliminating and fixing problems? I have often found myself in this hamster wheel in my efforts to remove problems, it seems the faster I work to conquer them, the faster more problems appear. It's as if they multiply.

I have since learned a new strategy with problems. I use them for my gain. I make lemonade out of my lemons. In *The Power to See it Through*, Harry Emerson shares, "There is a Scandinavian saying which some of us might well take as a rallying cry for our lives: (The north wind made the Vikings.)" The Vikings didn't see the wind as an opposing force; they saw it as the source of strength, an endurance building opportunity.

Where on earth did we get the idea that we need to remove or eliminate opposition and obstacles in order to obtain happiness and enjoyment? In the absence of difficulty, how would our strength be built? And when we obtain comfort and ease are we ever really happy anyway?

Instead of trying to get rid of your problems, leverage them to your advantage. It's a mindset switch from living in defense, to living in offense. Living in defense is exhausting. Change your position and switch to offense. Turn every minus into a positive and make lemonade from life's sour lemons.

# My Journal

_____

_____

_____

_____

_____

_____

_____

_____

_____

_____

_____

_____

_____

_____

_____

_____

_____

*Enjoy the lighter load of*
*shifting blame to responsibility.*

# 28. FREEDOM FROM BLAME

*"Take your life in your own hands and what happens? A terrible thing: no one to blame." ~ Erica Jong*

The weight of blame is much heavier than the weight of responsibility. When we experience emotions of blame does it matter if they are justified or not? To answer that question, let's take a deeper look at what blame is, how it shows up, and what it does to us.

Blame is basically pointing the finger at whom or what is at fault for a result or an outcome. Blame removes responsibility from us and puts it onto another person or thing, leaving us powerless. Blame can show up in simple, everyday situations such as, "Who moved my keys?" all the way to extremely complex and sensitive situations, such as, "Whose fault was the divorce?"

Blame can sound like this: "It's my friend's fault that I missed the plane. I'm late because my son couldn't find his jacket. It's the economy's fault that I lost my house. That student misbehaves because of his parents. My child got into drugs because of his friends."

Does it really matter if any of those statements are true or false? Does it really matter who or what is at fault? The time, energy, and emotions spent on blaming others only delays personal improvement and compromises the ability to move forward.

How does blame impact our lives? Because blame puts us in a place of being mistreated, it puts us into the role of a victim, powerless, waiting and hoping for someone or something to bring us the needed change. Blame stifles our resourcefulness and creativity. Blame cuts off our ability to take action. Thoughts of blame create a variety of negative emotions...feelings of offense, upset, frustration, betrayal, entitlement, jealousy, envy, anger, resentment, stress, distrust, fear, confusion, hurt, sadness...all of which dis-empower us to move forward towards growth and improvement.

So, how do we succeed in life, free from blame? OUR MINDSET. It all starts with our thoughts. Blame comes from a mindset void of taking responsibility. The way to overcome blame is by simply taking responsibility. Responding to situations with, "What can I do to improve this? What will it take to resolve this situation?" Build up your level of responsibility through your thoughts, through your inner dialogue. Make it a habit to respond to situations with, "What can I do? What can be done to move forward? Who would be willing to work with me overcome this?" Do you hear how these are all thoughts of empowerment that will get you into action? They are all thoughts free of who is at fault. They are thoughts that get you on with it.

I encourage you today to listen to the thoughts you are having around any situation. Are these thoughts putting fault on another or are they thoughts producing solutions? A strong positive mindset is rich in responsibility and it produces positive energy through curiosity, growth, creativity, humility, joy, understanding, abundance, peace, and prosperity. Choose responsibility and you will gain prosperity.

# My Journal

_____

_____

_____

_____

_____

_____

_____

_____

_____

_____

_____

_____

_____

_____

_____

_____

_____

_____

*Honor yourself and
create your happiness.*

# 29. HAPPINESS

*"Happiness is the meaning and the purpose of life, the whole aim and end of human existence."* ~ *Aristotle*

Where does happiness come from? There are many books out there that address this question. *The Happiness Project* by Gretchen Rubin is a really good one. The basis of most books on the subject of happiness share the same message, which is, happiness comes from within. Now if this is true, which I believe it is, what can we do to create more happiness in our lives?

One thing that is very important in having happiness is that you honor yourself. I recently realized I was a bit lacking in the area of having fun. I had been so preoccupied with work, responsibility, and taking care of things that I had neglected to have fun. So I made 2 lists. One list was for all the things that I enjoy doing, that are fun to me like socializing, going out to eat with family and friends, dancing, hiking, doing art projects, shopping and more.

The other list is for all the things that make me feel good after I've done them, such as yoga, running, cleaning my house, praying or meditating, and more. Those are things that aren't necessarily fun at the time, but they are an investment, that causes me to feel good about myself afterwards. I have made it a point to do one thing from each list every day. Since I have begun this, I have been much happier and enjoying my days more. I am happier and more joyful because I am honoring myself.

Where are you on your happiness chart? What are you doing every day to honor yourself? Make your lists of things that are fun and things that make you feel good and be sure to do at least one from each list. Honor yourself and create more happiness and enjoyment. You deserve it!

# My Journal

_____

_____

_____

_____

_____

_____

_____

_____

_____

_____

_____

_____

_____

_____

_____

_____

_____

# 30. SELF-IMAGE

*"When your image improves, your performance improves."* ~ *Zig Ziglar*

The thoughts we have about our self dictate how we see our self. Our thoughts create our self-image. Generally, we are our own worst critics and that is so destructive and sad. We could be our biggest fan and support, encouraging our selves to be our best.

Of all the ailments in the world, one that isn't addressed often enough is self-image. It is a priority to see ourselves at our best, in our full potential. Everyone deserves to have confidence, self-appreciation, and self-respect. It is up to us to develop those things.

It is good to recognize there are forces working against us having a positive self-image. Whether it be other people talking down to your or our current media telling us our teeth need to be whiter, straighter and that our bank account needs to be bigger and safer or that our work needs to be faster, greater. Despite all the messages saying you are not good enough, smart enough, attractive enough, you must decide you are enough and you are perfect just as you are.

The greatest effort you can make to improve anything in your life will start with your self-image. When you raise your self-image and confidence everything else will increase. We are too often focusing on the symptoms, instead of the root cause for our situation. So, if you have desires or goals to improve any external or circumstantial area of your life, start with your self-image about it and the rest will follow.

What are you doing today and on a habitual basis to invest in your self-image? One thing you can do is write truths about yourself, then read them out loud. Truths such as, "I am great. I am smart. I am strong. I am creative, fun, beautiful." Replace any thoughts of, "I can't" with "I can." Remove any messages or people that tell you otherwise. You may end up with a new set of friends. You are worth the change. Decide today that you will choose thoughts and friends that create a more positive self-image and experience the rewards in every other area of your life.

# My Journal

_____

_____

_____

_____

_____

_____

_____

_____

_____

_____

_____

_____

_____

_____

_____

_____

_____

*Develop the habit of appreciation
and abundance will follow.*

# 31. APPRECIATION

*"I would rather appreciate things I can not have, than to have things I cannot appreciate."* ~ *Elbert Hubbard*

Appreciation is a habit you can develop. It is a choice. In Dale Carnegie's book *How to Win Friends and Influence People* he talks about how appreciation doesn't just come naturally. It is something we must decide to create in our hearts. Think of children, when they start talking, they don't naturally say, "Thank you for feeding me and thank you for changing my diapers." We teach our children to say, "thank you" and to appreciate.

Knowing this, we can let go of the expectation of receiving appreciation from others. I have found myself, in the past, thinking, "He didn't even say thank you," or "You'd think she would have appreciated my effort." With the knowledge that appreciation requires intention, it is perfectly understandable for someone not to acknowledge or appreciate our efforts. After reading Dale Carnegie's book, I have stopped expecting appreciation from others and when I receive appreciation, it is a treat.

Though I do not expect others to be appreciative, I have decided to develop the habit of appreciation for myself. Everyday, I write down 10 things I appreciate. This habit causes me to notice more things to appreciate. The rewards for this habit are huge. It has greatly impacted my overall mindset and attitude. It creates in me more positivity and keeps me out of pity parties.

Just yesterday I was cleaning my house, and started having thoughts and feeling irritated about how I wish I had a bigger, newer home, so that we weren't all crammed in and cluttered and almost instantly appreciation rose in me and I responded by thinking of all the things I appreciated about this house, like our small mortgage, less to clean, it's cute, we have a garden, pretty flowers, we live in a cul-de-sac, near a park and on and on my appreciation grew. I felt happy.

Appreciation creates joy, happiness, and abundance. When we appreciate what we have, we create room for more to come in. Write down 10 things you appreciate today and make this a daily habit. Watch how easy it is to appreciate more each and every day.

# My Journal

*Write a new song today.*

# 32. CREATIVITY

*"But out of limitations comes creativity."* ~ *Debbie Allen*

Creativity is birthed in an environment of obstacles. Without problems, there is no demand for creativity. Think of what creativity does. Creativity transforms, it reinvents, it re-purposes and improves. Life is a certain way and then creativity comes in and increases it. Obstacles and change open the door for creativity. However, to tap into it, you must be willing and open. To be willing and open, you must see those obstacles as opportunities and inspiration to create.

One myth about creativity is that some people are creative and others are not. This is simply not true. We are all creative beyond measure. This myth is often created from the misperception that creativity is expressed only through the arts, the obvious vehicles of music, writing, dance, etc. Those expressions are just a few of the endless variety of ways to tap into creativity. There is potential for creativity in ANYTHING — creativity with numbers, organizing, ideas, systems, computer programs, sports, and much more. Creative expression is endless in variety.

What is your creative ability? What is your creative outlet? You have many, I'm sure. Whatever creative expressions you have, know this, they are one of a kind and they will grow when you use them. So, when problems show up, look at those problems as the stage for your creativity to perform. Most of the world's greatest inventions were created because of a problem. My husband is a songwriter and when he accidentally hit the wrong chord it inadvertently created some of his best songs.

What wrong chords have been struck in your life? What new songs will you write? I encourage you today to respond to obstructions and obstacles with creativity and serve the world something new.

# My Journal

_____

_____

_____

_____

_____

_____

_____

_____

_____

_____

_____

_____

_____

_____

_____

*Let responsibility produce freedom of choice.*

# 33. RESPONSIBILITY

*"You must take personal responsibility. You cannot change the circumstances, the seasons, or the wind, but you can change yourself. That is something you have charge of." ~ Jim Rhon*

Responsibility is such a beautiful thing. I didn't always feel that way about it. In the past, when I would hear the word responsibility, I would think, "Yuck, boring, heavy-burden," and, "No thank you." But now that I have enjoyed the lighter load responsibility brings, I wouldn't live any other way.

One of the best things about responsibility is that it doesn't waste time. When we live from a place of responsibility, we don't waste time or energy looking for who is at fault. We simply look for and find a solution, then get on with it. Responsibility creates a great sense of empowerment, no need to sit and wait around for something or someone outside of us. Because being a person of responsibility causes us to be resourceful, we are able to contribute, serve and be a great team player and leader.

Thinking from a responsibility mindset puts you in the driver's seat, allowing you to easily handle any problems in our life, family, and work because having responsibility creates choice in any situation. Responsibility responds to difficulties by thinking, "How can I contribute to solving this?" One of the things that I have enjoyed most by living from a place of responsibility is how easy forgiveness and compassion have become for me.

There is no space or time for complaining. Where there is complaining, there is lack in responsibility, so when we live responsible lives, free from complaining, it inspires and encourages others to do the same. You will notice responsible people attract other responsible people; complainers attract other complainers and so on....

Choose to live your life from a place of responsibility. Create an environment of responsibility and enjoy the freedom, enjoyment and lighter load it creates for you.

# My Journal

_____

_____

_____

_____

_____

_____

_____

_____

_____

_____

_____

_____

_____

_____

_____

Live in your one of a kind expression
& enjoy your priceless value

# 34. VALUE

*"There is something in every one of you that waits and listens for the sound of the genuine in yourself." ~ Howard Thurman*

Where does value come from? Supply and demand. When supply is low, demand goes up. Therefore, when something is rare it has more value. Now think about yourself. What is your value? HOW VALUABLE ARE YOU? To answer this, consider the fact that you are one of a kind. The truth is you are priceless.

For the world to experience your priceless value, you must live in authenticity. Are you living in your one of a kind expression? Are you using your one of a kind gift? You will know if you are because you will be seen as rare, as valuable and there will be a demand for your value.

Too often we compromise whom we are to fit in and conform to the average. Every time we do that, we dilute and minimize our authentic expression, which dilutes and minimizes our value. Lack of authenticity reduces our options tremendously. Living vanilla lives, going with the flow, working to fit in and avoiding rocking the boat, all restrict our one of a kind abilities. That way of living is not only boring, but it robs the world of what we truly have to offer.

Where in your life are you holding back and limiting your one of a kind value? How would your life be different, if you were to step into your 100% authentic expression? One of my favorite scriptures is, "A man's gift will make room for him." That is so true. Every time I am courageously living in my authenticity and in my values, doors open up and opportunities arise. My income increases, my options are many and life is so easy. The contrary is true as well. When I conform, I get stuck. My options go away and my value goes down.

If you desire greater income, increased happiness, and a truly fulfilling life, step into your one of a kind value. You deserve it and the world needs it.

# My Journal

_____

_____

_____

_____

_____

_____

_____

_____

_____

_____

_____

_____

_____

_____

_____

_____

_____

Stop making delays on what you can do today. Get into action now.

# 35. ACTION

*"Inaction breeds doubt and fear. Action breeds confidence and courage. If you want to conquer fear, do not sit home and think about it Go out and get busy." ~ Dale Carnegie*

What is stopping us from taking action and stepping into our full potential? Our thoughts! Our thoughts, on autopilot, keep us comfortable. They tell us things that would stop us from taking action and stop us from doing what we can now. "I'm not qualified yet. I need more experience. Am I allowed to?" All these thoughts delay us from doing today what we can, telling us we have to wait for the green light.

Harriet Tubman was a woman, who did not let her limitations or obstacles stop her from doing what she could. You probably know her as the woman who, after escaping from slavery, into which she was born, saved hundreds and thousands of slaves during and post war. What inspires me deeply about her is that as a child she was beaten severely and in one beating suffered a head wound, causing her disabling seizures, narcoleptic attacks and headaches. Despite these ailments, she made a huge difference in the lives of countless people. She didn't wait for the certificate of completion, giving her the right to go free the slaves. She didn't think, "Oh, there's nothing I can do, since I could have a seizure." She took action. She did what she could with what she had and that was clearly enough. Her efforts saved thousands.

I am so inspired by her because I do find myself making excuses why I can't do something. "I'm not allowed. I'm not ready." What a lie! There's always something I can do right now, with what I have.

We all have potential. We all have ability. We can all do something right now with what we have. Let's shift our focus off what is stopping us and onto what we can do. I encourage you today; take a look at your situation and ask, what can I do, right now, with what I have? Take action and move forward.

# My Journal

*Make room for all that you
desire in your life and world.*

# 36. PREPARE

*"Change is the essence of life. Be willing to surrender what you are for what you could become."* ~ Anonymous

Have you ever bought a new refrigerator or new furniture? Upon purchasing, you schedule a time and date for the delivery. You go home and what do you do? You move out your old items and make room for the new to be delivered, right? When you think about your new furniture, you feel excitement. You even picture how you will position the furniture. Maybe you even buy some new accessories-pillows, candles, and curtains to match. The bottom-line here is that you MAKE ROOM and PREPARE for the new.

So, how does this relate to other areas in your life? For a tree to continue to grow properly, it has to be pruned. The old, dead branches need to be cut away, to make room for new growth. The same is true for us. If we are to fit something new into our lives, we must make room for it. Everything takes up space, visible or unseen; it is taking up space. Whatever you desire may be right in front of you, at your fingertips. But if there is no room for it, it can't come in.

What is taking up space in your world that if removed, would create space for the new, for that which you desire? It could be a mindset of fear, doubt, and worry that can be replaced with creative, refreshing, positive thinking. It may be in your finances. You know debt takes up space. So get rid of the debt to make room for the abundance, for the savings, for the prosperity. It may be a relationship. It may be really simple, like some new clothes. Go through your closet and get rid of all the clothes that have dust on the shoulders.

Whatever it is that you desire, tangible or intangible, make room for it. Create the space for it. Then PREPARE for it.

# My Journal

_____

_____

_____

_____

_____

_____

_____

_____

_____

_____

_____

_____

_____

_____

_____

_____

Get out of your comfort zone.

# 37. STRETCH

*"One's mind, once stretched by a new idea, never regains its original dimensions." ~ Oliver Wendell Holmes*

Have you ever watched a child try something new? Children are fearless. They see something that interests them and they go for it. My nephew Drake started baseball and watching him swing that bat was something else. It didn't matter how many times he missed the ball. He would just swing again. He just kept trying until he got it.

What happens to that child like effort, that eagerness to continue trying, and that freedom from concern regarding what we look like? The older we get, the more care we put into looking good or being right. The need to look good and be right really holds us back from trying new things and learning new things. I've been reading a great course book called *The Artist's Way*, which helps you to tap into your creativity. In the book it talks about how we can't look good and get better at the same time. That statement is exactly what causes us to get stuck and stagnant and to stop progressing. We get too caught up in looking good.

Think back to a time you learned something new, maybe how to ride a bike or swim. When was the last time you learned how to do something new? Chances are in the learning process; you may have looked silly for a bit, but looking silly allowed you to learn something new. What is it that you would like to learn how to do now? Play the piano, water ski; speak in front of a crowd. Whatever it is that you would like to learn, I encourage you to GET OUT OF YOUR COMFORT ZONE and do it. STRETCH YOURSELF. Don't worry about looking good or being right, just get out there and do something different!

Take a moment and write down a few things you would like to learn that you know will be a stretch for you. Then write down what actions you must take to go for it. Schedule them on your calendar and do it. Stretching and learning new things will create exhilaration, fulfillment, confidence and growth. Get out of your comfort zone and enjoy what it brings you!

# My Journal

Take action to
pursue your dream.

# 38. UNLEASH YOUR VISION

*"Start writing, no matter what. The water does not flow until the faucet is turned on." ~ Louis L'Amour*

Each of us has untapped potential on the inside, sitting there, waiting to be released. What is your vision? What is your dream? What would it take for you to unleash that vision? The quote above reveals deep wisdom and truth. You've got to take action and open the door, so that greatness can unfold.

One thing I have realized through coaching so many amazing people is that fear too often stops us from taking action and fully committing to a goal or dream. It has been through helping my coaching clients break through this obstacle that I have also recognized how it shows up in my own life.

Playing it safe, staying in our comfort zone, and watching and waiting for the right time can sadly cut off the flow of our dream. Tip toeing towards our goals and dreams can be deadly. Please hear me. I am in no way discounting the necessity of planning and preparing. I am saying that once you have completed your due diligence, there comes a point where 100% full-on commitment is necessary to the birth of your dream.

Have you ever met someone new and asked, "What do you do?" Then they answer, "I do a lot of things. I do _____ to pay the bills, but my real passion is _____." Do you ever notice that most people do their real passion on the side, almost as a hobby, hoping that one day that part-time hobby will magically become how they spend their days? It's the "waiting until I retire" syndrome.

What is your passion? What is the part time hobby you wish you could do full time? What would it take for you to take action and make the commitment to materialize your vision? Life is short. I implore you. Believe in yourself. Believe in your dream and make a commitment to unfold that vision.

# My Journal

_____

_____

_____

_____

_____

_____

_____

_____

_____

_____

_____

_____

_____

_____

_____

_____

*You will never know what your limits are until you push them.*

# 39. EFFORT

*"Only those who will risk going too far can possibly find out how far one can go." ~T.S. Elliot*

Half way through a yoga class, I was exhausted, fully exerted. I had been giving it my all from the very start and we were in a particularly difficult pose, when the instructor asked that we go into a handstand. Almost instantly I resolved to hold the pose I was in, instead of trying to go into the handstand. I already knew what my limits were. Knowing that I am not able to do a handstand fully rested, there would be no way I could do one when my upper body was already exhausted and weak.

As I waited while others worked on their handstands I thought to myself, "How do you know you can't do one? When is the last time you tried?" I couldn't remember the last time I tried and thought, "I guess I won't know until I try." So, I tried. I attempted to get up on a handstand about 5 or 6 times. In my attempts, I surprised myself. I wasn't able to get all the way up but I got pretty close; closer than I thought possible.

That surprise produced in me excitement and a sense of conquering. I felt proud of myself for trying. That one physical act of pushing myself and testing my limits in the middle of a yoga class, in what seemed to be a typical routine in my week, had a great impact on me. It provoked more thinking in me. I began to consider what other areas in my life do I hold back on? Where am I simply not trying due to a belief that I can't? What other areas have I been sitting back and limiting myself?

Now, what about you? Where are you holding back? Where in your life can you attempt something that you see as impossible? When is the last time you tested your limits?  A key indicator for whether or not you are stretching yourself is: how often do you surprise yourself? If you are testing your limits, you are learning, growing and undoubtedly surprising yourself. It doesn't have to be a physical action. It could be in another area. Maybe there's someone you believe you could never forgive. Maybe there's a conversation so tough, you think it's impossible to have. Whatever it is that you see as impossible, take a stab at it. Because the truth is, you don't know until you try. Make the effort. And regardless of the outcome, make it a habit to give your all and make an attempt towards achieving whatever it is that you want!

# My Journal

*Step out of competition
and into creativity.*

# 40. COMPETITION

*"Focus on competition has always been a formula for mediocrity."* ~ *Daniel Burrus*

Competition only exists in our mind. It really is just an illusion that limits us from becoming all that we are. Though competition can be motivating for a period of time, it is not sustainable because of its roots. Competition stems from comparisons, which take our attention outside of our self and away from our unique abilities. Competition is really a limiting energy that thrives on scarcity and the need to exceed another. The reality is that our unique, one of a kind abilities cannot be compared to the next person's unique, one of a kind abilities. This is why competition vaporizes in the presence of authenticity. It simply cannot exist.

Authenticity stems from abundance, creativity, and unique expression. It runs on inspiration, making it sustainable for a lifetime. World-renowned athletes, actors and performers achieve exceptional levels of success from their authenticity and inner drive, not competition. Mikhail Baryshnikov, known as one of the 20th century's best dancers said, "I do not try to dance better than anyone else. I only try to dance better than myself." It is possible that in his early days, he may have been competitive with other dancers, but for him to have achieved his untouchable unique expression and sustained success, he had to turn away from competition with others and into his connection with his unique ability.

We all know what competition feels like and how it temporarily motivates us. If your drive is currently coming from competition, I encourage you to step out of it and into authenticity. Don't run on competition, which is short-lived and surely diluting your unique abilities. Shift that attention inward. Tap into your unique expression and experience the freedom and abundance from authenticity drives. It is an inspiration that is sustainable and cannot be competed against.

# My Journal

_____

_____

_____

_____

_____

_____

_____

_____

_____

_____

_____

_____

_____

_____

_____

_____

Take courage.
Take action.

# 41. COURAGE

*"There are risks and costs to action. But they are far less than the long range risks of comfortable inaction." ~ John F. Kennedy*

It's so much easier to fully commit to a decision than it is to safely take baby steps towards it. That is the typical thought, only after the action has been made. Often times we will vacillate over something for so long before taking action and when we finally get moving, we wonder, "Why didn't I do this sooner?" It takes courage to get into action. Too often, we are waiting and hoping for everything to be ready and prepared to take action and that day never comes. We must use our hope to develop our courage.

Most often, the door in front of us won't open, until we close the door behind us. One of the worst places to be is in limbo, in the safe zone, in the land of good intentions, the place where every thing is fine, but not great. We are hoping and waiting for the right timing to step into our dream, but it feels risky, so we wait. Andy Andrews talks about how an undecided heart stops you from taking action and robs your life of fulfillment.

You know that saying, "When one door closes another one opens." You see the order? First the door closes, then the other opens. Too often we are waiting for a door to open before taking action. Many people live their lives waiting for the door to open, but we must recognize when it is our time to take action. It's that place of fearlessness when true courage takes over and you fully commit your heart and the actions follow.

Where in your life are you playing it safe? Where are you holding back from putting in full commitment? Access your courage. You have it there, available for use. With courage you can do anything you choose. No more playing it safe. Take courage. Take action. You will be so glad you did!

# My Journal

Plant compliment seeds
abundantly every day.

# 42. COMPLIMENT SEEDS

*"Everybody likes a compliment." ~ Abraham Lincoln*

Our words create. Once a word is spoken, it is like planting a seed in the ground. In time, that seed will grow and produce. What type of seeds are you planting? What type of words are you speaking? Are you planting seeds that will grow into beautiful and bountiful flowers or are you planting seeds that will grow into weeds?

Take notice to the words you are speaking about yourself and others. Make the decision to spread compliments throughout your day. You never know what the affect one of your compliments will have on another person.

The habit of giving out compliments is something you can develop. All it starts with is a decision to pay out compliments. You may want to start with those closest to you, and then increase it to one stranger a day. You may make a game of it to see how many compliments you can give in a day. Just by making the decision to give out compliments, you will begin to notice more opportunities to pass them out. When you notice something to compliment, speak up. Just say it. Paying compliments is one of the most effective and rewarding ways for you to increase appreciation and abundance in your life. Watch and see how it makes you feel. Watch and see the other person's face brighten up.

Send compliments in a hand written note or e-mail. Those are treasures. I save all my compliments. I have a file folder filled with handwritten notes people have given to me over the years. I also have a folder in my e-mail called Compliments. I often go back and read the encouraging words people have sent me and it always picks me up and inspires me. Save the compliments you receive in a file or in your inbox folder, to access for down days. You will be amazed at how much joy and hope they bring you.

There's no better way to increase your joy, happiness and prosperity, than to be generous with your compliments, so plant compliment seeds today!

# My Journal

*Create an environment that
helps others be their best.*

# 43. HELP

*"Few things can help an individual more than to place responsibility on him, and to let him know that you trust him." ~ Booker T. Washington*

Create an environment that brings out the best in others. This is certainly easier said, than done. However, once you develop the habit of lifting people up and bringing out their best, your world will be transformed. "Be the change you want to see in the world" is a famous quote by Mahatma Gandhi. It spells out how you create the environment that helps others be their best.

People show up in line with the thoughts and emotions we have about them. Our thoughts and our words are not only creating our environment, they are creating the environment for those around us. When we think, speak, and expect the best out of others, we make it easy for them to be their best. We set them up for success. The opposite is also true. It works both ways. When we think, speak and expect someone to be rude, grouchy, and uncooperative, that's exactly how he or she will show up. We set them up them for failure.

Creating an environment for others to be their best can be most challenging for people who have let us down or disappointed us in the past, but those are also the ones you can best serve by expecting and believing in them. Take a moment and write down the name of someone you would like to see in his or her full potential. Now write 10 sentences seeing them at their best. Write down what you will feel when they show up in their full potential. Keep that vision and expect that greatness for that person. That is how you create the environment that will make it easy for them to be their best. You treat them as if they already are. You draw it out of them.

We are all able to create a positive environment if we choose to make it our priority. Let's do our part and make it easier for others to be their best and watch how others will do the same for you. This is how we all rise to the top and help each other.

# My Journal

_____

_____

_____

_____

_____

_____

_____

_____

_____

_____

_____

_____

_____

_____

_____

_____

_____

_____

*Create motivation in any area of your life today.*

# 44. MOTIVATION

*"People often say that motivation doesn't last. Well, neither does bathing-that's why we recommend it daily." ~ Zig Ziglar*

We have all experienced lack of motivation in one area or another, whether it is in our health, a relationship, work, whatever the area, when we find ourselves saying, "I'm just not that motivated," know it can be changed very quickly. It is actually really simple. I have a formula for it, and I'll share a personal experience in how I use it.

I have not felt very motivated to exercise consistently. My workouts have been sporadic and I have had to use will power to do what minimal exercise I have done. So, to find motivation, the first thing I will do is find my hope. "How would I like this situation to be? What am I hoping for?" "I hope I will enjoy and want to workout." Hope opens up possibility. Hope awakens our "want to." Then I ask more questions to grow my hope into a "want." "What if I wanted to workout more consistently? What would that feel like? What would that look like? What would it take for me to want to work out consistently?" Just pondering these questions, gives me ideas and grows a vision. Once I start to see the vision of what it will be like and look like when I exercise consistently and enjoy it, I have my vision. I can imagine what it will be like. That get's me excited about it and bam — there's my MOTIVATION. I want to get into action now from that motivation. See how easy it is.

Now you try it. Use the steps below on any topic that you are lacking motivation.

1.  Choose to hope for whatever you need motivation in. Choose it's possible.

2.  Find hope. What are you hoping for?

3.  Awaken your "want." What do you want it to be like, look like, and feel like?

4.  Grow the vision. Keep writing or thinking about what you want it to be until that vision is crystal clear.

5.  MOTIVATION: When the vision is clear, the motivation shows up.

6.  ACTION: You will feel compelled to action from your motivation.

If you are lacking motivation in any area of your life, it can be changed, just by believing it is possible, activating your hope, awakening your want to, and igniting your MOTIVATION. It starts with a willingness to hope. Are you willing to hope?

# My Journal

# 45. CAPABILITY

*"Treat people as if they are what they ought to be, and you can help them become what they are capable of becoming."* ~ *Johann von Goethe*

Throughout my life, I have too often found myself consumed with worry and concern over a loved one or friend. I have too often jumped in to offer help and advice, only to exhaust my resources — mental, emotional, or tangible. What I have learned and experienced again and again, is the truth that people are CREATIVE, RESOURCEFUL and ABLE to solve their own problems. They are honestly better and more capable of resolving their problems, than me or anyone else.

Unfortunately, we don't always see others, especially those we are closest to, in their full potential. It is evident when we worry about them or feel the need to jump in and "help." When our thoughts around our loved ones start with, "he should, she needs to..." you can rest assure, those thoughts are not coming from our great wisdom and desire to help, they are coming from our belief that the other person is incapable or that we know better. These thoughts and beliefs come from our judgments. One definition of the word judgment is an, "an opinion or an estimate based on observation." So, you can see how easy it is for us to observe someone's situation and go down the Judgment Path if we are unaware of the value in going down the Believe the Best in Others Path.

So, why believe the best in others? Why believe that others are CREATIVE, RESOURCEFUL and WHOLE? Because it empowers that person instead of limiting them. When we believe and expect the best in others, they rise to the occasion. When we have confidence in their abilities, we give them the necessary space to tap into their resourcefulness, instead of jumping in to fix it, which robs them of their opportunity to grow and to ultimately build up their self-confidence. After all, resourcefulness and creativity are birthed in times of lack and need.

Try it this week. EXPECT THE BEST IN OTHERS. SEE THEM AS **CREATIVE, RESOURCEFUL AND WHOLE.** Do this in both your thoughts and actions and watch those around you unfold their true potential. This is a gift to them. It is a gift to you.

# My Journal

*Let encouragement fuel you and those around you.*

# 46. ENCOURAGEMENT

*"Correction does much, but encouragement does more."* ~ *Johann Wolfgang von Goethe*

Encouragement gives life, energy, and motivation. You really cannot over do encouragement. We all need it. Encouragement can be the difference maker for those around you. One hand written note, one kind text message, and a quick call of encouragement can all go a long way.

I make it a point, every time I can, to encourage everyone around me. One of the best ways we can encourage others when they are down is by asking "what" questions. When you ask questions that start with what, such as, "What would it take?" You are telling that person, they can do it. There is opportunity. You help them think of their own solutions, which is much more impactful than you telling them what you think they should do. As they come up with answers, respond with encouraging words, like, "great job." I know it may sound elementary to tell someone they are "fantastic" or "terrific" but encouraging words are powerful.

Physician George Adams found encouragement to be so vital to a person's existence that he called it "oxygen to the soul." You hear that? "Oxygen to the soul." Oxygen is the difference between life and death and encouragement could be the difference between life and death of a dream, of a hope, of a plan.

Take advantage of every opportunity to encourage someone. Take notice of things you appreciate. Build people up with encouraging words and by asking "what?" questions. Extend admiration and appreciation for even the most mundane thing, such as, "thank you for getting the mail" or "You made a great dinner" "Your smile brightened my day" "That shirt looks great on you" Praise a person every time you see any improvement. Again, that is fuel and life to them.

Encouragement has a compounding affect on others and on our self. When we encourage others, we naturally begin to encourage ourselves. Remember, "Encouragement is oxygen to the soul." Be generous with your encouragement today!

# My Journal

_____

_____

_____

_____

_____

_____

_____

_____

_____

_____

_____

_____

_____

_____

_____

_____

_____

# 47. ANCHOR THOUGHTS

*"Drag your thoughts away from your troubles... by the ears, by the heels, or any other way you can manage it. ~ Mark Twain*

Our thoughts are like anchors, keeping us in one place. If you want to change your current situation, change your thoughts. Take a look at your current situation and listen for the thoughts you are having around that circumstance. Chances are your thoughts and beliefs support your situation. So, how do we change our thoughts and create improved results? It starts by considering what we are putting in. What music are you listening to? What are you watching? What conversations are you having? Who are you hanging around? What books are you reading? The answers to those questions are the influencers currently affecting your thoughts.

Improving our thoughts is just like improving our health. If we were to exercise several hours a day, but continue to put in more calories than we were exerting, we would not see improvement in our health. The same is true with our mindset, if we are filling our minds with negativity, it won't matter how many affirmations or positive books we read. Because our thoughts are like anchors, it is crucial to understand that worry is a form of meditation that cements our circumstances. Do not engage in worry or fill your mind with things that will provoke worry.

Take a minute to consider:

1. What are the anchor thoughts, keeping you in your current situation?

2. Create new anchor thoughts that support your desired circumstance.

3. Identify your current influencers- (Music, friends, TV, books)

4. Which influencers do you choose to remove and replace?

It is up to us to choose what we allow in our minds. What we see and hear affects our thoughts and attitude. If we want to have a positive mindset, we must be selective with what we allow in.

# My Journal

_____

_____

_____

_____

_____

_____

_____

_____

_____

_____

_____

_____

_____

_____

_____

_____

*You have plenty of time to accomplish all you intend to do.*

# 48. TIME

*"Until you value yourself, you won't value your time. Until you value your time, you will not do anything with it." ~ M. Scott Peck*

Just like money, and just like water, time is a resource. The way we look at time and what we believe about it will determine what we can do with it. Do we believe we don't have enough or do we believe we have plenty? Do we believe time is on our side or do we believe time is working against us? Take a minute to write about how you currently view time. What do you think about time?

"I don't have enough time."

"I have too much time on my hands."

"I need more time."

"I wish time would go by faster...slower."

Whatever you believe about time is creating your relationship with time. What if you were to see time as perfectly what you needed? What if you were to believe, "I have plenty of time to accomplish all that I intend to do"? How would your day be different? How would you feel about time? What would you do with your day, seeing time as plenty?

Sometimes we use the excuse of not having enough time to stop us from doing what we can. Other times choose to believe we have too much time to be happy. Rarely have I heard someone say, "I have just enough time to be, do, or have all that I want."

The truth is time can work for us, if we choose to view it as so. It is a choice. It is a belief. Decide today that you will see time as perfectly what you need. Choose to believe you have plenty of time to use; however you choose to use it. Don't believe the lie that you don't have enough time. When you begin to see time in abundance, as more than enough, you will use your time more efficiently and more wisely.

# My Journal

_____

_____

_____

_____

_____

_____

_____

_____

_____

_____

_____

_____

_____

_____

_____

_____

_____

*Contribution creates abundance.*

# 49. CONTRIBUTION

*"Strive not to be a success, but to be of value." ~ Albert Einstein*

Where is your focus? Is it on survival, on your own wants and needs? Naturally, yes. Without effort, we do focus on our own needs. It takes an effort to shift that attention off us and onto others. What happens when we shift our attention on contributing to others? We create both abundance and fulfillment and ultimately, our needs get met. In the midst of our needs, how can we shift our attention onto others? Well, it starts by considering, "What can I contribute and who can I help?" Contribution is a mindset. It is a way of thinking. Despite your needs, there are always others that you can contribute to.

I have been in some form of a sales capacity most of my career and I have experienced contrasting sales energies. One is the energy to make sales, to hit goals, to accomplish my focus and my gain. The other is much more rewarding and productive and that is to be in an energy of contributing to others. Zig Ziglar's quote; "If you help enough other people get what they want, you will get what you want" is so true.

In the process of using our resources, gifts, talents, and strengths to better others, without effort or attention, our needs will be met in abundance. It simply takes a decision to turn your attention to others and develop the habit of contribution. It is a way of life free from scarcity and abundant in blessing.

Let go of scarcity. Let go of the thoughts and concerns of how your wants and needs will be met and put your energy into contributing to others. Abundance and prosperity will overflow in every area of your life. It is a spiritual law- give and it shall be given. Just like gravity, what goes up must come down, when you contribute to others, your needs will be more than met.

Take a moment right now and answer the following questions. What can I contribute and whom can I help? Then take action. As you contribute to others, watch your needs be met in great abundance.

# My Journal

Influence occurs whether
we notice it or not.

# 50. INFLUENCE

*You can never really live anyone else's life, not even your child's. The influence you exert is through your own life, and what you've become yourself."* ~ *Eleanor Roosevelt*

I received a surprise package in the mail recently that had a deep impact on me. The package came from a friend Rusty, who I hadn't seen in over a year; someone I met through business and quickly developed a respect and fondness for. The package included a book and a handwritten letter addressed to both my husband and I. The letter was a complete and total surprise, filled with encouraging and affirming words for what my husband and I have been building in both of our businesses.

I was so touched to read his kind words and was taken back at how much Rusty had noticed about what we were doing. This gesture of kindness and affirmation provoked my attention on two levels. One is in how Rusty affected me and two is how Stephen and I affected Rusty. This is how powerful influence is. We never know who will be impacted by our lives. We never know who is noticing what we are doing and who we are.

Somehow, someway, while Stephen and I were going about our journey of courage, authentic expression, and entrepreneurship it clearly had an impact on Rusty and compelled him to express that to us. His willingness to express and encourage us has given me reassurance and encouragement to fuel me to continue on and follow my heart in my journey for purpose and contribution.

I am in such amazement at the connection and influence we all have on each other, whether we are aware of it or not. Who we are and what we do really does matter. It is being witnessed. It is influencing and impacting others. Whose lives are you influencing? Take a moment to consider who is watching and being influenced by you. Now, who is influencing you? Take notice because influence is occurring, in even the briefest moments. One act of kindness is being witnessed by onlookers and then re-told to many others, potentially hundreds, thousands, and with social media millions. So, I encourage you today take notice of your life and your decisions. Have courage to follow your heart and your dreams. It is not just about us fulfilling our dreams. It is also about those watching, witnessing, and being inspired to fulfill their dreams. When we follow our heart, we are encouraging others to do the same. Be like Rusty, willing to share your words of encouragement and affirmation to others.

# My Journal

_____

_____

_____

_____

_____

_____

_____

_____

_____

_____

_____

_____

_____

_____

_____

_____

# 51. CHANGE

*"We must be willing to let go of the life we have planned so as to have the life that is waiting for us." ~ E.M. Forster, British Writer~*

Most people do not invite change. In fact most people resist change. One reason for this is discomfort. Any change, even change for good, is uncomfortable. One way that we must invite and accept change is through letting go. I love the above quote by E.M. Forster. Too often we are holding on so tightly to something in our minds that we miss what we have in our hands. Yes, we form our plans and we work towards achieving our goals, but we must be ready and willing to let those plans go for the greater. Don't get stuck in determination.

In recent days, I have found myself transitioning from a place of force and domination to a place of power and presence. When I reflect on my life I can clearly see the difference. I am grateful that I had such a drive to accomplish and overcome, and I am even more grateful now to be experiencing my drive in a whole new light, coming from a place of patience and with a solid knowing that allows for acceptance. This is a change for me.

I am 32 years old and if I could sum up the main lesson I have learned so far, the lesson is patience. Patience is power. Patience is strength. Patience is the change I have finally received. I can remember when I first started realizing that I needed to develop patience. I would feel dread and resistance, not wanting to have to develop patience. I wanted to go, go, go and get, get, get. I felt that if I was to have what I wanted, I must go and get it. That way of thinking produced a lot for me. Some of it great, some of it was heartache. It certainly exhausted me and finally brought me to this wonderful place of surrender.

I look back in great appreciation at the most difficult and most challenging experiences and know those experiences aided me in my ability to change. I encourage you today, whatever change is needed in your heart and in your life, though it may be uncomfortable, accept it. Change it is necessary for growth. Lou Holtz has been quoted "you're either growing or dying--'maintaining' doesn't count."  So, which would you prefer? I am certain you will choose growth and therefore, embrace change. Allow change in your heart and mind and watch your beauty unfold.

# My Journal

*Last week of the year.*

# 52. REFLECTION

This is an excerpt from my diary. It reveals my perspective at the end of 2010, having come out of several years of growth and change. I hope this inspires you to allow life's challenges and difficulties to be the ingredients to your triumph, happiness, and wisdom! Happy New Year!

*December 21, 2010 - The past couple of years have generated both tremendous loss and priceless gain. From March of 2008 and the months following, several major losses affected my world- It began with the loss of my marriage and all that it provided me- the false sense of security of a future, hopes, and dreams, followed with the loss of my sister-in-law and my uncle, the loss of income and career compounded to the loss of all that comforted me. My entire world had crumbled and I had no vision for my future. The need to care for my children kept me focused on survival and gave me the drive to work past it all.*

*And somehow over the last couple years, despite the losses and disappointments, the pain and uncertainty, as I end this year and reflect I realize that I have actually gained so much. My heart is strong, rich with hope and gratitude for all that I have gained. What I have gained is priceless and cannot be purchased. It cannot be negotiated because it is free, it is mine, and it has given me true prosperity.*

*I have gained perspective, awareness, and clarity. I am very certain of who I am, what I deserve, what I want, and I'm confident in my faith. Fear has lost its power over me and my trust in God has given me a peace and a freedom that I have always longed for. And through the losses, I had no other choice, but to become conscious of the reality that life is precious and fleeting and there are no guarantees or entitlements. Certain things are permanent. Certain things are out of our control and no matter how hard we try, sometimes it is impossible for us to reverse that which has been done or said. Results and consequences of this sort can either break us down or improve our lives. Overcoming loss and growing from the grief requires both our effort and the touch of God. Sometimes just breathing was my effort, other times reading an inspirational book was the effort, other times switching my focus on helping someone else was my effort, sometimes choosing to be grateful for what I did have was the effort. Through the efforts and with God's "magic wand" I have learned how to accept that which I cannot change, find hope, look on the bright side and grow and learn.*

*I learned that everything that I really need and everything that actually matters cannot be obtained through effort or purchase. It is just there, free, in me. My life and my existence are where it begins. My loved ones are gifts, gems and precious. I am not entitled to them and I am not guaranteed to get to keep them, therefore, I must show them my love and enjoy them all I can while they are in my life. Those who we treasure most are the easiest to take for granted the easiest to lose sight of as priorities, if I allow my focus to be distracted on other things. The tragedy in doing that is when the irreplaceable is lost or taken. In keeping this awareness, I am committed to living the rest of my life in simplicity, able to enjoy and love those that matter most. That's the way to prosperity and true happiness. **Happy New Year!!!***

# My Journal

# About Corry Inspires

Corry's coaching and speaking events ignite motivation and create inspired action to:

- Improve mindset

- Increase authenticity

- Create balance & fulfillment

- Produce independence & freedom

- Clarify vision

- Generate desired results

Explore the possibility of coaching for you or your company. Corry Inspires Coaching offers Executive, Team, and Individual coaching programs.

Have Corry speak at your next:

- Conference

- Sales or staff meeting

- Networking event

**Sign up for your FREE Monday Motivation at:**

**www.corryinspires.com.**

Contact Corry:corry@corryinspires.com or 916.343.2068

**For more information visit: www.corryinspires.com.**

Made in the USA
Charleston, SC
07 September 2011